_101 W(_
awaken
to appl; ... ..., g.....g y.. a
positive outlook on everything you want, think, or do.
Anyone can relate to this book, and I would
recommend that everyone take advantage of its
powerful insight.

Derek Brown
Tight End, Oakland Raiders
National Football League

As a television news anchor and health reporter, I
realize healing the spirit is every bit as important as
healing the body. Turn to any page of Ashley Kohly's
book and you will discover a new way to soothe your
soul. This wonderful book reminds us of the lessons in
life we must never forget, and teaches us new lessons
that will add enrichment and enjoyment to everyone's
existence.

Barbara West
Television News Anchor

101 Ways...is an enlightening, comforting group of
ideas and beliefs which will inspire you with it's
insightfulness yet intuitive simplicity. It will fill your
heart and soul with a sense of warmth and goodness,
and enable you to achieve balance in your life. It
teaches you how to find peace and happiness dealing
with difficult emotions and situations from your past,
present and future. _101 Ways_...is motivating and
uplifting and these are words everyone should strive
to live by. In short, it's "a recipe for happiness."

Edward Guindi M.D., F.A.C.O.G.
Advanced Women's Health Specialists

This book will help many people take note of their blessings. Those they have and those that are yet to come. It is highly motivational and it makes us deeply grateful for the gift of life.

Senior Pastor Joel C. Hunter
Northland Community Church

101 Ways is a sure-fire way to find balance in your life. It soothes life's anxieties.

S. Guindi
Prudential Transact Realty
Broker/Owner

Morsels of wisdom…nicely packaged and ready to eat. Enjoy!

Brian Campbell, Ph.D.
Christian Psychologist

No one can tell someone else how to live, what to believe, which choices to make. But we can share some of the insights and lessons we've learned, the signposts that have marked the passage of our own lives. This is what Ashly Kohly's book offers: fuel for the journey, light on the pathway of each seeker's private spiritual quest.

Ronnie D. Clemmer
Feature and Television Movie Producer

Thanks for your inspirational book. You certainly hit on all the key issues of life.

Rich DeVos

*101 Ways To Add Joy
To Your Life!*

*Through Spiritual
Awakenings*

101 Ways To Add Joy To Your Life!

Through Spiritual Awakenings

Ashly Kohly

A straight 30% of the net proceeds goes to homelessness-your brothers and sisters in the Lord. In your walk of your life always keep in mind, we are all God's children trying to work together, feeling and dealing with each other.

101 Ways To Add Joy To Your Life!
Through Spiritual Awakenings

Preface

This book is to be a mirror for you.
I want to help you see your inner child,
your beauty, your thoughts,
your words and your actions.
You're put on the spot–
you come out of the spot,
and through you
God will make the difference.

Dedication

This book is dedicated
to all the angels that go
the extra step to love others.

Acknowledgment

This goes to all the children of
Christ that went the extra step
to love and show me better how to
have more humility in all things
and to seek truth which is Jesus,
without whom there is no life at all.

To my mom who is one of the best
examples of pure unselfish love,
who constantly gives love –
not some – but all she has.
To my dad who's insight and
wisdom has kept me seeking.
To my brothers Mark and Mario
because that while we all are learning
how to love each other better we are
constantly growing closer.

To Grandma Ellenburg who always
cared about my salvation.

To Lisa Ellenburg who's encouragement and unconditional love has always lifted me up.
To Diane who introduced me to Northland Church and gave me the option to sneak out if I didn't like it.

To Joel, the pastor there, for always maturing us in Christ, Mark D. for always being my buddy and helping me to understand God's nature, to David, Capt. Kirt, Jenny, Patty, Scott, Ed, Johnny, Big Dog, Ingrid, and to all of those that have loved me through the different phases of life, although I may have been hard to love, to help teach me God's way, which is love and truth.

To Gabriel Vaughn and Legacy Publishing for doing an unbelievable job of walking me through the publishing process.

Contents

This book is a compilation of
thoughts, beliefs, and triumphs
over the last 14 years, through God's
love, prayer, grace and mercy reveals
certainties and absolutes that we all
encounter in all of our lives...

In our busy day-to-day life
we tend to fade away from the simple.
This book is designed to be quick
contemporary reading, daily
inspirational applicable food for the
soul, a fresh breath that at any page
will bring you back to Spiritual basics
in leading you down the proper path.

Proverbs 1:7a The fear
of the Lord is the beginning
of wisdom.

Fearful

First decide if it's really fear
that's stopping you or if it's something
that isn't morally right to do.
If it's really fear that's stopping you
from something that is great
for you in your life,
understand one thing: fear is usually
☞ **False Evidence Appearing Real.**
If what you want is God's way,
find confidence in your heart;
let him be your guide;
strive even harder for your dreams and
they will never be denied.

Psalm 23:4 "I will fear
no evil for you are with
me.

Lack Of
Attention

Pay attention; focus on one thing;
realize whatever is in front of you
is there for a reason; understand it;
learn something;
give something you love
your undivided attention.
God gave us two ears and one mouth,
so we can listen more than we talk.
You can't learn something
if you're not paying attention.

James 1: 19(b) Be quick
to listen, slow to speak
and slow to become angry.

James 1: 22 Do not merely
listen to His word; do what it says

Timid

What are you timid about?
Is it your job?
Pursuing something, or someone, new?
Find something to believe in;
○ build your self-esteem; with the Lord.
▲ start a work out program;
learn to love yourself first; Him 1st others 2nd
● let the Lord guide you in prayer, 3rd
and go for what you know
with confidence and shine

2 Timothy 1:7 God does not
give us a spirit of timidity,
but a spirit of power, of love,
and a sound mind.

4

Education

Education is not just to prepare you
for life, it is a continuing part of life.
Learning is a journey, not a destination.
It comes to us in many forms—
school, life experience, reading and
soul searching. All of these combined
help make us as individuals.
Remember, all the knowledge
in the world is not written down.
Knowledge in every form helps us
to succeed. Always take advantage
of a learning opportunity.

Proverbs 1:5 Let the wise
listen and add to their
learning

Complacent

*Complacent reminds me of "lack of"!
What do you lack? Are you complacent
in your work, personal relationships, with
yourself, with family? Whatever it is, you
just have a **lack of a goal.** So I tell you
now: choose your goal and move forward!
Stop what you're doing, think about what
you are complacent about and get a piece
of paper. Think about where you would
like to be if nothing was stopping you.
Then as fast as you can write,
take one minute and jot down each
aspect of your life as you choose it to be.
Then reread your dreams and get to work.*

Phil 3:14
I press on toward the
goal to win the prize
for which God has called
us heavenward in Christ
Jesus.

6

You Live Your Life In Darkness

What is surrounding you that
is not enlightening you?
🪶 Seek and you shall find it.
Most importantly,
invite Christ into your heart
and He will enlighten you!
⚫ Positive is light, negative is dark.
You can't see in the dark!
⚫⚫ Run from—**and I mean run from—**
people, places, habits
and things that are negative.

Peter 2:9 But you are a
chosen people, a royal
Priesthood, a holy nation, a
people belonging to God.. the
that you may declare the
praises of God who has called
you out of darkness into
His marvelous Light

Negativity

➤ Don't ever let yourself get caught up with
  negative places, people, or things.
  It can only subtract from you.
  Through God's love you can reverse
  the negatives to positive.
• The quickest way to kill negativity is with
  a _positive thought_, _word_, _or action_.
  Remember there are _only_
  two forces in this world:
➤ _positive and negative; good and bad_.
  Bad is only a deterioration of good.

Ps. 119:105
Your word is a lamp unto
my feet and a light unto
my path.

Words
To Live By

Get good, say good, stay good!
Instead of complaining,
condemning, and criticizing.
Compliment, uplift and encourage!!!

Deut. 6:5 Love the Lord your God with all your heart, soul & mind. And love others as yourself.

Feeling Unloved

*God says the quickest way
to receive love is to give love.
We can never repay Him for all
He has done and all the love
He has given us,
He already possesses
all of the universe and it's contents-
so what can we possibly give to Him
that He doesn't already have.
**He says, "If you want to love me,
give love to others."***

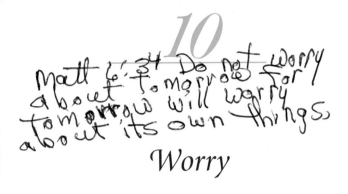

Matt 6:34 Do not worry about tomorrow for tomorrow will worry about its own things,

Worry

Doesn't it seem that the
vast majority of the things you worry
about or fear don't ever actually happen?
The other things you can't do
anything about anyway.
Your best bet is just to pray for
God's love and protection in Jesus' name;
and know God is always there for you,
guiding you through everything.
He is **always** with you!

Is 26:3 God will keep
him in perfect peace whose
Mind is stayed on Him,

Searching For The Answer

We are all made in the image of God.
Allow God into your heart and you will
have the means to find the answer.
Everyone possesses the answers
*to all adversity **through God's love.***
To find the truth or the solution
you're searching for take a look inside.
There is where you'll find the answer!
Your <u>mind</u> is where truth can <u>lie</u>.
Your <u>heart</u> is where truth <u>lives</u>.

Jealousy

Who are you jealous of?
What are you jealous about?
Why are you selling yourself short?
What is it about yourself
that you are not secure with?
Answer this and focus on
what's in your heart.
Spend time building yourself into the best
you can be; **be kind to yourself.**
Give love to the person
you're jealous of and stand in truth,
knowing that when God created you,

1 Corin 13: 4(9)
Love suffers long
and is kind. love
does not envy

He made you exquisite-
with beauty in His eyes, seeds of
perfection, and a heart of light,
goodness and love.
Take what He gave you, and
**instead of focusing your energy
on someone else -**
**take that powerful energy
and give it to yourself.**
You'll see the illuminating
results you can create!

Looking For Direction

Find something <u>deep-seeded</u> in <u>your heart</u>.
A place you want to be in your life.
Close your eyes; picture it; believe in
what you see, bring it close to you.
Put yourself in your future;
know it's your present leading you there;
make it bigger; give it color and sound!
Make it even larger;
believe in what you see.
Make a goal to get there - write it down!
Think of things that will give you the
results you want and what you need
to do to get there. Lastly, **get moving!**
Now you've <u>found ~~direction~~</u>!

Genesis 1:27(a) So God
created man in His
own image.

Stereotypes

*Just as God <u>created you to be
unique and special</u>,
He created others to be unique and
special. We are all God's children and
He doesn't love one child more
than the other because of
inconsequential values (height, beauty,
success, money, color, age).
He loves all of us for the wonderful love
and joy we spread in our lives,
and finds the best in each of us.
* <u>Find the best in yourself</u>
<u>and encourage the best in others!</u>*

Eph. 5:19 Speak to one another
in psalms + hymns + spiritual
songs, singing and making melody
in your heart to the Lord.
    Phil. 2:4 Let each of
you look out not only
for his own interests,
but also for the interests
of others.
Giving thanks

Feeling Sad

Give joy to another!
A compliment, a kind word,
gesture, gift, or flower
(especially if you pick it).
By giving happiness to another,
you receive indescribable
joy in return.

Be thankful for what
you have. Eph 5:20
Ps. 95:2
Be content,
Eph 5: 20(a)
Give thanks always for all
things to God the Father
in the name of our Lord
Jesus Christ

Thinking Of All
The Things
You Don't Have

You will never receive the things
you want if you're focusing on the
things in your life that you don't have.
Start counting all the people, things,
and other blessings that you **do** have
to be grateful about in your life.
By walking with a grateful heart,
you leave yourself open to receive
all the things that you don't have.

Doubt/Gossip

If someone is creating doubt in your heart,
or mind, especially about someone you
love, cherish or care about, know
one thing: Truth is good, gossip is not.
People can, and probably always will
bring things to you for a reason, not
meaning to do harm. But ask yourself
questions like "what is the reason?"
"What's the motivation?" Where are they
really coming from? There may be no
truth to what they are saying. Do not
engage or encourage that person
in more gossip, because it only creates
a whirlwind of negative energy.
Thank them, and go on with your day.

• <u>Look to God, and you'll always know the truth</u>. Every day the foundation of life is being built in your heart for a reason. Don't let "neggies" chip away the good thoughts you have for someone that really is a truly good person because you're doubting them. Secondly, don't create more doubt in others by gossiping more, hoping to find the "real deal."

The answer: go to the source you doubt and address it with confidence, love, and respect. Then, if you're still unsure - pray! "When in doubt - pray!" The truth is what Christ is about, and the truth is what you'll always receive if you will only ask.

Happiness

*Happiness seems to be something we all
strive for in life! Whenever you ask
someone what they want, inevitably they
answer, "To be happy!" That's great!
What does happiness mean to you?
Prosperity? The love of your life? A great
body? Spirituality? Which one? It's all
of these! Everybody strives to do well
financially, but if you don't have your
health, all the money in the world will not
make a difference. We all strive for health,
but if you don't have other goals,
or direction, how are we going
to become interesting, motivated people?*

If you have the love of your life without
God's guidance or the good health
to be with them, will love last
as long as it is meant to?
**So they all work together
(God, health, love, and achievement)
to form a balanced life.**
Strive to be the best you can
in all areas of your life.
Stay fit; keep expanding your goals,
and be passionate in whatever you do.
**Focus your eyes on Him
and your priorities
and the happiness will follow.**

Loyalty

*Loyalty is one of the greatest strengths
that you can possess!* **Don't be scared
to stand by what you believe in!
Your beliefs are held for good reason.**
*If you're evaluating why you should
believe in anything anymore,
look for the truth.*
*Pray that God reveals to you what He
wants you to see, and stand by your guns!
If you feel you truly have nothing to stand
by anymore, then continue to look for
truth and stand up for what you know.*
**Remember being loyal is one of the
greatest gifts you can give!**

Cheating On Someone

Why are you scared?
Define the answer. **Find out where
in your past you were hurt.
Forgive it so you can heal it.**
Why do you think there is
someone out there that can
give you more than the one
God has presently gifted you with?
**If the person in your life is not the
one that is meant for you;
then have dignity, courage and love
for the other and allow them to go
and be free.**

Continued

If you have found someone else,
be honest with yourself
and be truthful about what you want.
Let them go, so they can begin to heal.
Don't create more hurt that
they will have to heal later.
To end a relationship means that you're
not cheating yourself or them,
you can walk away from the situation
in truth and not lies.
If you are dishonest, you are not only
cheating them, but you are cheating
yourself and foiling your destiny.

Mental Infidelity

*Not only can you have physical infidelity
away from the one you love,
but infidelity can take many forms.
Mental infidelity can be anything from
constant flirting to giving your spare time
and attention to someone else, when you
could be sending positive energy to the
one you love. Infidelity can involve
playing mental games, being distant, or
being more passionate about areas of
your life that don't add up to Eternity.*
**So, love the one you're with!
Give them the love, respect and
attention they need and deserve!**
Pay attention to things that are lasting.

Anger And Violence

"Anger and violence will always be the
longest road to resolving anything."
Don't let negativity get the best of your
communication with someone.
**Remember you can usually
attract more bees with honey!**
Slow down; stay positive; take a minute
to really evaluate the situation,
then approach whatever it is
with love and fairness.
Above all, stay present tense and
mentally positive. You'll get a lot more
accomplished in a shorter period of time,
not to mention gaining
a little respect for your maturity.

Complaining

*There are only two basic emotions -
positive and negative, love and hate,
or good and bad.*
**Negative is a deterioration of positive;
hate is a deterioration of love;
bad is a deterioration of good.**
*Complaining is negative!
Think of all the good in your life and
things you should be grateful for, instead
of complaining about your situation.
Find the answers.
If you're going to do any talking at all,
talk about a positive solution.
It's conversation that's more worthwhile.*

Forgiveness

*Has someone done something to you
that wasn't the right thing to do?
Don't condemn them, or delight in evil
thoughts - that's not what you're about!*
Give it to the Lord. *Remember,
"'Vengeance is mine,' sayeth the Lord."
We are all here to learn and grow in
this journey into our Father's arms.
Forgive your brother or sister and give it
to the Lord. There are so many other
things in life that need your energy.*
**Remember you can not truly live until
you forgive. Then you are truly free!**
*Remember Shakespeare's words,
"To err is human; to forgive divine."*

Mental Abuse

It's ironic that **the people that get the most mental abuse from us are the people we supposedly love.** Stop that! Stop trying to find ways to get someone's goat, or game play until you get the action or reaction that you wanted to prompt from the one you love. Tell them to stop also! Give love and encouragement; get to the heart of matters. If you have a dispute, stay focused and not proud. **Remember that it's the one you love, so stop playing games, there is never a winner!** The truth, love, understanding, and forgiveness are the only places solutions reside!

Low Motivation / Vision

Open your eyes. Search your heart.
Find your dreams and go for them!
Set your sights high!
Make sure it's part of God's will.
Make a plan of action; start to write it
down. A vision will start to crystallize.
Start to make a realistic time table;
follow through. Go for what you know.
Keep going until you get there.
Be persistent! *Don't ever quit*
until you're where you want to be.

*Whether it's spiritual understanding
you want, mental growth,
physical fitness, or financial stability;
let determination guide you!
Take action! Don't ever give up!
Are you starting to see what I mean?*
**If you want things to change
in your life, you are the only one
who can change things!**
*So get going! If you keep
doing what you're doing,
you'll keep getting what you're getting.
Get it!*

Dieting

There's no such thing!
Guys and gals, fitness and health is not
a fad or a fashion; it's a way of life!
Don't make a goal to go on a diet,
make a commitment to eat better,
healthier, lighter, or less.
Do you want this awesome physique?
Then right now get a picture -
a picture of what you want your body
(your waist, hips, thighs, arms)
to look like.

Freeze it in your mind!
Shut your eyes, bring it close to you,
believe in what you see,
and with God's help,
you will achieve!
Make a strategy on how to get there;
and remember, you're forming the
rest of your life, so go easy on yourself!
The key is consistency!
Fitness is not a fad or a fashion,
it's forever!

Health

Good nutrition and exercising are
important aspects of health;
total balance is another.
**Good health is an infinite by-product
of mental attitude, which is a definite
by-product of spiritual well being.**
Caring, compassionate, positive,
Christ-like thoughts toward yourself
and others promote good health.
Remember, Christ is the beginning
and the end to enhancing your physical,
as well as overall, well being.

Focus

If you really want to penetrate
a goal or achieve a dream,
focus is the main ingredient.
It's kind of like this:
you can go outside and feel the sun
warm your face, or you can take
those same sun rays, force them
through a magnifying glass,
and start a forest fire.
It's all about channeling your energy
through emotions, attitude, and strength
to put the blinders on and look toward
the goal you trying to create -
and then going for it!

Lies

*If you're lying, you are unsettled about
something. Find out what you're not sure
about, get sure, get your facts straight
about whatever situation you're in, and
guess what:* **The truth will set you free!**
*Tell the truth at all costs. Remember, if a
man builds his castle on sand, it can be
washed away. If a man builds his castle
on solid foundation one brick at a time,
it will last forever! What can you lose by
telling the truth? Except something that,
in and of itself, can not be true.
Honesty is always the better policy.
By not lying, at least you know
you're always being true to yourself!*

Disrespectful

Get some manners!
Always show respect to everyone!
Young or old, wise or green,
slow or fast, happy or hurt, you should
always show respect to another.
There's almost no greater
compliment than to show respect and
kindness in any circumstance.
Always let someone finish
their thoughts before you speak,
always take into account
other's feelings and circumstances,
without judging.

Continued

*Take into consideration
someone else's views,
time and decisions they make.
You don't always have to
agree with them, but always try to
show respect at **all times to all people,**
even if they don't live up
to your expectations.
You never know, at some point in life,
you may not live up to
someone else's expectations and
you'll be happy when they give
you the same kindness in return.*

Distancing Yourself From Others

Why would you want to distance yourself? Is it for peace, a private thought or to regroup? **Okay!** *However, if it's to shut yourself out from others that are positive in your life, or maybe have a little more wisdom than you, then,* **don't!** *The Lord puts people in our life for a specific reason. Usually, it's to inspire, teach or share with them; or for them to inspire, teach, or share with you something, that, in the end, is good for you in your life. The Lord is teaching us through each other.* **God uses you to teach or share something wonderful in another's life, so don't shut out a person who could be blessing yours.**

33

Inconsistent

Be consistent in every thing
you say and do.
If you want to build things
that are lasting, be constant
in things that are good.
Always say good things,
have good values and good ethics
*and **stick to them!***
If you want to build relationships
that have trust, confidence,
loyalty, and devotion -
be as consistent as possible in all ways!
Be repetitive! Repeatedly give love!
Be consistent!

Flaky

How can people in your life
benefit from you in any spiritual,
positive or inspirational way
if they don't know
what ground you stand on?
**Remember, if you don't stand
for something in your life
you'll fall for anything!**
Be decisive, stand firm so
you can make headway,
so, at least you can be a positive
inspiration in another life
instead of a corn flake.

Investments

*Your only worth in Heaven is
equated to how much you constantly
loved one another on Earth –
all the other stuff you can't take with you.
Whatever you say or do,
make sure you're leaving a positive
investment in people. Those are the best
investments in this life.* **Always leave
people better than you found them.**
*That way, you're always
investing in the right stuff.*
**Don't worry,
God will handle your returns!**

Change/Growing Pains

Life is an ever refining process,
so get used to it!
You are the only one
in all of creation that has your
set of talents and abilities.
You're unique, rare and special, and in
all rarity there is the greatest of worth.
Although God loves you just
the way you are, he loves you too much
to leave you the way you are.
Everything He does is for
your own enhancement and good.

Failure

When things blow up - go bad -
as they sometimes do, stop and look!
Look closely at the situation from the
beginning and ask yourself one question:
**Was I wasting my time,
or was this God's will?**
If it was God's will, then your path
would bridge to a new beginning not
leave you with many pieces to an end.
**Remember, the Lord will never shut
a door unless He opens another.**
So never treat any situation with finality,
without exploring all positive options
that can surround you.
Sometimes God will let you stumble,
but He won't ever let you fall.

Purpose

*Life is really much simpler when
we realize -* **life is our orientation
to God.** *Our purpose on Earth
does not revolve around money, success,
our body, how much we know, how
perfect we are, or our own selfish desires.
Within your small time line of life, if you
ask Christ into your heart, follow Him
and know He is your Savior, your Lord,
Provider, Corrector and Protector,
you have served your purpose on Earth!*
**All the rest is gravy and
all the rest shall pass,
He is the only thing that is
eternal and that will last!**

Finding Individual Purpose

God's purpose for our lives-
once He's in your heart, your purpose
is revealed to you as you go.
"Life is our orientation to God."
Go as far as you can see and then you
can see further. Other than prayer how
can we get closer to knowing?
Look, listen, ask, question,
learn, build a relationship!

Look - at the patterns in your day
and how they compare to
how Christ would want them.

Listen - To what He wants for
your life, what you say, and
others' words of wisdom.

Learn - from the Bible,
your mistakes and others' victories.

Ask Questions Like:
What did I do today to strengthen
my orientation to Him?

What did I learn today about my limits
before I handed it over to God?

Who did I love today as You love me?
Who did I encourage today as You
encourage me?

What did I learn today that was fruitful?
What did I contribute today?

Continued

God says, "Rely on Me daily,
look at Me daily." Look for thanks,
things He has done and worked in
your day. He wants to see what you do
with your day, how you handle things,
surprises. When you contribute the little
things it makes the biggest difference
because God builds from the little things,
they make the biggest difference.
Trust in God with all of your heart,
give all things to Him! Pay attention to
what God does in your life everyday.

**You'll soon see your purpose -
The big picture!** The secret to progress
is to do what you do really well
on a daily basis with the right values.

Taking Responsibility For Your Actions

*Not taking responsibility for any part
of one's life is in denial of the present
tense, fogged by a part of their past,
and uncertain about their future.
You see, when someone can take a stand
for what they perceive is accurate
or right, even if it is not, then at least
you have a starting point to go on.
Avoiding responsibility is
avoiding the challenges God put
before you that day to learn from.
Stand tall and take responsibility
for what you do.*
It is the only way to be truly free.

Confronting Yourself

Why are you running?
What is it in your life you feel
God can't fix, solve, or heal?
He is with you in whatever
you do, think or feel.
Do not forget that even when
you think He's not there, He is.
His hand is in whatever situation you're
in, take the weight off, give it to Him,
put it in His hands. We can not run from
ourselves, or our situations, whatever is in
front of you give it to Christ so you
can be free of it. **Trust in Him.**

Sometimes, we can't see far enough in
front of us to see the real meaning
of how some things that seem unjust
unfold in life, but He can.
Don't waste your time running
from yourself or a situation via drugs,
alcohol, etc. He'll always bring
you back around the block
to reface the same challenge.
It's easier just to give the situation to Him,
even if you fear the situation.
"Do not fear things of this world,
for I have already conquered the world."

Living In The Past

Why are you sitting in the past?
**You're living in the past because
you're scared to embrace your future!**
*Heal what you're holding on to,
forgive it, and then let it go.
Don't be scared for all the magnificent
things God has in store for you—
look forward!*
**Life's like driving a car—
you can't go forward if you're always
looking in the rear view mirror!**
*Make sure you're looking ahead,
only glance back to stay on coarse
and to keep the right direction!*

Set Backs

Sometimes what seems like
God's little set backs,
are really just little blinks of time
where it's His way of giving you
His point of view to review.

Exhausted In Achievement

Success does have effort attached!
To achieve something of great significance
requires significant thought, planning,
vision, dedication, desire and grace.
Strive to be the best,
but take time to recharge too!
Remember something average
doesn't take that much energy.
So be happy you're tired;
you're probably succeeding!

Indecision

Ask yourself if what you're about
to do or say would be OK
if Christ were standing
right next to you.
What would he think?
*Would your **mom** be proud?*
Now any decision you need to make
should be a little bit easier!

Sin

*If anything is taking you away
from the **relish of God**
or His commandments,
the true beauty of who
He created you to be,
or the joy another has for the day -
to you, this is sin.*

The Right Values

To find your values, be real.
Determine what's most
important in your life.
Do it in order of priority.
Then you will see what you value.
You will also see what you
*value **the most.***
*To find **good** values,*
ask how much of what
you listed will last you until eternity?

Net Worth

Worth can be calculated
a few different ways.
But with "Real Worth"
we can sum up the total pretty quick:
A man's worth is determined not
by what he has in this life,
but rather what he **is,**
and how much **real** love he gave
unselfishly to others.

Being Your Physical Best

There is no magic formula.
A great body is just a
by-product of hard work,
focus and eating right.
Work out hard, get determined
and eat healthy, and over time,
like with every other goal,
small miracles begin to happen.
Work plus faith equals results.

Rejection

What sometimes feels like
rejection is really connection!
Sometimes we feel rejection because things
aren't meant to be for us in our life.
Don't fight it. Then again, sometimes it
can also mean that persistence pays,
so you try until there is
understanding or a result.
The difference is that either way,
God knows this is your opportunity to
practice faith, look to Him and listen.
**There is no need getting stressed out
over things you can't control!**
And if you listen closely,
you'll hear the truth.

A Reason
To Love

*Don't ever love others
because of what you think
they can do for you,
but what God can develop
in them because of you,
and in you because of them.*

At The End Of The Day

It's not how much we accomplished in this world that will ultimately matter. **It will be how much we loved all those people that were tough to love.** *Sometimes that is God building strength and understanding within you. Even if you never see a result, your results are seen by God and you will have a blessed treasure stored up in Heaven! He says, "if you want to love me love others."*

In Disguise

The best returns in this world
are not made up of this world, and
investing in people is extremely difficult.
Because people are uncertain,
selfish, crabby, you know –
sometimes just like you.
Invest in people,
because God invests in you.
Everything else will
come to pass or perish.

Life Without God

It's simple!
God is what centers us,
if you don't have Him as your center,
no matter what you achieve,
sooner or later,
you're going to be off balance.
And with God as your center,
no matter what you achieve or
don't achieve you're always going to be
solid, right, on target
and where you're supposed to be!

Do No Harm!

Religion tells us not to murder,
but in essence God tell us
not ever to kill or hurt
anything in any way!
Try to do things in this life
that will **promote life and**
help others to shine at their best.

Inner Light, Inner Calm

*One way to have light on something
is to ask yourself,
"What would Jesus do?"
Know one thing - you can't do anything
spiritual or beautiful for Christ when
the energy you're projecting is
anger, negativity, hostility, or slander.*
**Practice humility,
somehow it just always
puts things into perspective.
Remember love is strength!
Take into account
all that you should be grateful for.
Calmness is power!**

Unanswered Prayers

You know the old saying,
"Some of God's biggest blessings
are unanswered prayers."
But also know if what you're asking for
is meant to be for you in your life,
and you're following God's divine laws
and love, then always remember
and never forget that your
Father in Heaven answers your prayers.
Have faith, be patient, and remember,
God is never a minute early nor
is He ever a second late.

Projecting

*Positive projection through everything
we think, say, feel, do,
we are constantly projecting emotion,
thoughts, feeling, and energy.
This world is made up of energy -
every bit of it - and most everything is
coming to or going away from.*
**So whatever you project out into
the universe usually comes
back to you in one form or another.**
*So project great things, and by divine law,
receive the projection of positive
things and energies to you.
You usually always get what you project!*

Hearing
The Holy Spirit

Someone told me once,
"If I had realized a long time ago that my
intuition was mostly the Holy Spirit,
I would have been a lot further
in life with less mistakes!"
Be quiet, stop over analyzing,
be still in your instant thoughts that
come from nowhere, and listen to them.
Follow your gut.
Think about it, have you ever
known something before it happened
but didn't know you where right
until it had already proven itself?

Continued

For example, driving down the road
and you knew that there was a policeman
ahead, but you didn't slow down, instead
you had a close call or got pulled over.
**Know that the Lord saves us from
things in our day that we will never
know about.** So, when you feel that little
whisper in your ear, or feel that it seems to
be God's will - follow it! Because in these
lie the seeds of the habits Christ
wants us to develop on a constant basis.
We all have daily insights!
You can see more clearly sometimes
if you just open your eyes
and pay attention without looking.

State Of Mind

Everything is a state of mind.
We can not control what other people
will say think feel or do, or how
they will act or react to things.
We just have a choice of whether
we fill our minds with positive loving
things or negative clouded emotions.
If you keep your spirit and soul
intact, your mind will follow!

Charity

It's the key to Heaven!
Always give to give, this is God's way!
Giving to get is not true giving.
Don't ever think about whether
or not you should or shouldn't give
something to someone; it's not up to
you if a person is deserving or not,
that's for God to decide.
Just by the mere fact that God laid the
thought upon your heart to give means
that is not your gift to keep anyway.
Fear not what you give away,
even words from your heart;
God sees and hears everything you do
and say and He will always give
back to you, not the same, but "ten-fold."

Perfect Will And Permissible Will

We all sometimes hold on to stuff
in this world too tightly, including people,
and when God needs to take it
out of our hands it hurts.
God has a perfect will for you
and He has a permissible will.
We might think we're happy with our
permissible will, but if you're not
living the plan God has for you,
then you're living in the "okay" of life,
and missing the **awesomeness** of life!
That's life at it's best!
**We can't mess up God's plan;
remember, He's God!**

Avoiding Possessiveness

Even when you're married,
you don't own the other person.
So, in turn, if you don't own it,
it's not yours to possess.
Protective is good.
Possessive emotions usually lead to doubt.
Only God can possess,
so it's all in His control anyway.
Live and just let live.
Just love and you will promote
what you want - which is love.

Death

Is there really such a thing?
Of course there is!
I hope I die daily because I know that
I can not truly live and see God
until I (ego) truly die.
There is death of attitudes, habits,
mind-sets, and sin. The Lord says,
"We can not truly live until we die."
When we are concentrating
on ourselves, we are
at the lowest vibration of living.

64

When we are caring for others,
we are at one of the highest vibrations
of our soul and of life.
Then, there is death of the physical,
which is just clothing around our soul.
Try to be Christ like, so your soul
will be better for Christ to keep.
Remember life is just a journey
into your Father's arms,
so just always remember
the big picture, which is eternal.
**The "You" that is in
Christ will never die.**

65

Self-Destruction

Do you know how long it took God to create you? Me neither! But the point is you are fearfully and wonderfully made, with seeds of perfection to Him, and beauty in His eyes. It takes us too long to build ourselves up; don't go and tear it down, or let anyone else, for that matter. **What is it within yourself that makes you want to destroy what He's given you?** *No matter what it is, the key is to find it, because it can be healed. From smoking and excessive drinking to drugs and wanting even death - they are all self destructive and all healable. Search deep, find the root, then do one thing - believe with all your might that God can fix it.* **Pray, ask, mean it and receive!**

Grumpy

Decide what you are grumpy about,
write it down.
Lift your arms, take a deep breath, smile,
think of all the blessings in your life.
Smile even if you're so grumpy right now
that you can't think of any blessings!
A smile sends positive signals
to your brain and
you will feel happiness.
Keep smiling or laughing
until you're not grumpy anymore.

Nagging

Be solution-oriented and understanding!
Instead of nagging about something,
try to understand
the other person's viewpoint.
If something is bothering you about
a situation, get to the root of
the aggravation, remembering also that
any relationship is a compromise.
Stay positive and find a solution.
No one ever added an hour to
his or her life by non-communicative,
unproductive, negative nagging.
Give love, support and understanding
just as you would like in return.

Stress Control

*Don't try to make up that hour
you lost all day! Don't sweat the
tiny things; focus on the big picture!
Keep your priorities in focus; write down
what you need to do. And be honest
with others, you can only do the best you
can do.* **Put your energy toward the
things in your control.** *If people would
just spend more time living in the present
tense and get concerned about the things
in their control, they would be a lot more
productive and joyful. The more you focus
energy on the things you have control of
the more you start to realize
there is no time to sweat the stuff
you don't have control over!*

Good
Perception

*Prayer, reading the biblical truth
(even Thomas Jefferson said,
"It's one of the best books there is"),
listening to yourself, learning from
your mistakes and others,
and living righteously in all things.
This helps to build a
clean basis for perception.
With all these you can improve
your perception, because your view
will be based on truth, not of this world.*

False Witness

Religion tells us don't bear false witness.
God would not want you to fabricate
in any way any part of your life.
No matter how successful you are,
if you want to get somewhere
in this life of real lasting significance
build your life and those around you
on strength and truth.
All the rest sooner or later will perish.

Adultery

The Ten Commandments tell us,
"Do not commit adultery."
Do not desire, go after, wish for,
or flirt with someone that
God has brought together in marriage.
You will always lose. The same principal
holds true for a person that has a
significant other of some sort.
Right is right and wrong is wrong.
Don't play a losing game.
God's way is the only way of truth.
For every girl there is a boy and
for every boy there is a girl—
don't take someone else's,
trust in what the Lord has for you.

Taking Away

The Bible tells us, "Do not steal."
Do not take away from anyone
or anything in this world
that is not yours to take.
This can mean anything from emotions
that don't belong to you,
that you yearn for from another,
to stealing praise from another
to parking spaces and promotions.
Just keep your eyes on the Lord and
He will supply all of
your needs and desires!

A Christian

Is a saint that's a sinner that's been saved,
as they say! Christ-like and still trying.
It's all about a relationship with him.
No goodie-two-shoes.
Wanting to do good is just a by product
of the relationship because you love Him.
Talking to Him (prayer) is starting
somewhere. It helps you build
a relationship. **You can't earn your
way into Heaven.**
It's a gift! A free one!
"No man can enter
the kingdom of heaven
except through My son, Jesus Christ!"
Right or wrong –
Is that a chance you're willing take?

Live For Today

*Take note of what you think about
and say. Choose words that are
present tense, that heal, that are positive.
What's in a man's heart is his destiny!*
**How can you ever move forward
productively without conflicts or
restraint if you live in the past and
don't even know it.** *When we put others
or ourselves in categories, or use
words that judge others or ourselves,
or measure others or ourselves,
we tend to be living in fear!
Embrace the crisp new present and with
your thoughts, create your own future.*

Stumble

If life were a football game,
God would play the blocking back.
He's there to protect us
and show us the way.
When we let him go in front of us,
we're protected. **Sometimes we run out**
into the field alone, thinking we can
handle it away from Him;
and we fumble. *The Lord may let*
you stumble and fumble until you learn
to stay close to Him, and follow His lead,
but He won't ever let you fall!

Pain

We all have it every so often!
This you can be sure of:
Time heals all things.
God can mend a broken heart.
What doesn't kill us makes us stronger,
This too shall pass.
Jesus really does love you, and
love really does conquer all,
especially if it's the love of God!

Balancing
Your Accounts

Not only repay every debt monetarily
before you leave this world.
Above all, ask for daily forgiveness
for the things that are not
pleasing to God
thus staying out of debt spiritually.

Laughing

Take time to laugh!
It's too short a day not
to smile loud,
it's positive food for the soul,
and positive energy for others.

Sarcasm

Some people may think this is cute,
or a nice way to communicate,
and some people get
their feelings hurt by it.
Funny is good, sarcasm is not.

Confessing

Unload, free yourself,
cleanse yourself, unite your hands,
give it to the Lord, renew yourself.
Walk in truth with God.
Doing wrong things to yourself
or others and not confessing them
to the Lord leaves a separation
between you and God.
Leave yourself open for Him to always
positively lift you up and help you.

Snobbery

*Reminds me of shallow hearts
and cloud-filled minds.
Are you so puffed that you live
on top of your heart without
understanding the depths of God's love?
When you die,
your only real worth in Heaven
was how much you loved one another.*

Ego

To have ego
of some degree is good,
to have the posture of Christ is better.

Impossible

First off, whether you
think in your mind you can do something
or you can't, either way your right!
Every thought you have,
positive or negative, opens doors.
Which door do you want to open?
The one with no possibilities
or the one with endless opportunities!
Above all, through Christ
all things are possible!

Renewal

You must rest not only your body,
but find time in the day
to rest your mind.
A time aside from when you're sleeping,
just to think of nothing and appreciate.
Find time to renew
your soul aside from when
you're praying and
just give joy to another.
To rest is to renew! To give is to renew!

Money

Money is not the root of all evil.
It's the ego and values centered
around the money that can be evil.
God gives to us to give to others.
Over the time line of life we may have,
and have not, and have again.
All money does is give us options.
Maybe one of your options is to do more
of the eternal things with what
God gives you, that will reap
true rewards in Heaven,
versus ego-centered things
that you can't always take with you.

Merciful

To know no mercy is
not to have understanding!!!
If you do not have a true
understanding of pain and compassion,
count on one thing being true:
It is better to be compassionate
than having to understand compassion
through your own pain.
God is merciful to you;
be merciful to others.

Treat Yourself

Remember the golden rule:
treat others the way
you would have them treat you.
If you don't treat yourself well,
then you don't know how to
treat others well.
Therefore treat others the way
Jesus would treat you.

Virtue

*The only true virtue is
that of an unaffected heart.
A heart that has no
preset opinions or prejudices.
We have often heard the phrase,
"As seeing through the eyes of a child."
If we could challenge ourselves daily
to attempt to see through
the eyes of a child,
to set aside opinions
and prejudices,
we could live the examples
God wants us to live in knowing
we come to Him as children.*

Humility

Humility describes
everything we should be.
To be humble, grateful, thankful, giving,
caring, and kind to others.
No matter how great you are,
everyone doesn't have to know it.
To have true humility is
to know that everything good
that happens in life comes from the Lord.

Healing

*If faith can move mountains,
in turn, you must believe
faith can heal.
True faith has no boundaries
and real belief knows
all God's words are true.*

Grounded

*God is our rock -
everything else is not.
Be rooted in God!*

Broken

*We all probably think if something
is broken, it's not as good as it was before.*
God is the perfect carpenter.
*Sometimes he allows us to break
in certain areas of our life
so we can mend by his will,
and with his skill,
to be created more like his image.
Sometimes something that appears to be
broken in the small picture was only
broken in order to become perfect and
to heal stronger in the big picture.*

Profanity

Cursing never impressed any one,
especially God.
So why include it in your vocabulary?
And just for the record –
God's last name is not damn!

Friends

*Eternity is not to long for friends
made in Heaven. You've heard
"those who pray together stay together."
True friends are a gift from God,
treat them as such.*

Saying Good-bye

*Remember, it's all in God's hands
and that's where it stands!
God sees our entire life.
He knows what you have been through,
and where you're going. He is the big
picture; so that's what you must trust in.
We don't always see the bigger plan.
You need not a sigh or a tear, everything is
in His hands for the good.*
All of our paths cross for a reason.
*All that is meant to be will be.
There is no "good-bye," just
"until I see you again."*
**We are all brothers and sisters
joined in heaven.**

Worship

Are you going to worship things of this
world that will not love you back?
Or that will rob you of the beauty of
who you are? Or that take away from
what you have purely to give?
Or that will rot away with time? If you're
going to worship, look up to, idolize,
or praise, make your efforts your light.
Worship the One that
gave His life for you, that would
never leave you or forsake you,
that absolutely loves you unconditionally,
and that will be with you eternally.
**There is one, and only one,
and this is Christ.**

Indulgent

*If you are constantly focusing
on things of the body, or the material,
can you really ever indulge in God?
It's not how much we fill our mind,
body and house with, but rather what
we're filling them with **that matters**.*

Judging Others

Only God sits that high!
Don't judge others for
you don't know
what purpose they serve.

Work

It's the price of success!
In every aspect of life -
friends, family, attitude, and ideas.
Work is the only way to get success.
So get used to it.

Wise Men

Very hard to come by!!!
But if they do,
stop and talk to them.
We need all the wisdom we can get.

The Conclusion

The secret of life is to enjoy the phases of life, wake up in the day with love in your heart, gleam in your eyes, and a smile!

The secret of love is opening up your heart. It's ok to be afraid! You're only here for a while, might as well show some style.

It's all a point of view, planets spinning through space. Try not to try too hard, you're just here for the ride. Walk with a grateful heart and leave everyone and everything a bit better than you found it. God loves you - let him lift you up high! The secret of life is enjoying the passage of time.

**That's where it stands.
It's all in God's hands...**

About the Author

Ashly Kohly is a fourth generation author. She is following a longstanding family tradition of sharing wisdom through authoring or public service. Ashly's great-grandfather was an ambassador to Spain, her grandfather founded the New York Credit Exchange and pioneered innovative industries in Europe and her father is a medical doctor focusing on new avenues of healing. Dozens of books on medicine, business, industry and politics have been authored by the Kohly family. Ashly herself has been an active volunteer in many charitable organizations and is the president and founder of "Foundation for LIFE," (Love Is Feeding Everyone). Ashly is also a fitness enthusiast having produced several aerobic videos. Currently residing in Orlando, Florida, she is an active public speaker promoting the values and lessons of life that have brought tremendous joy to herself and many others, which she has captured in her first book entitled, *"101 Ways to Add Joy to Your Life."*